Twoism

twoism

Ali Blythe

icehouse poetry
an imprint of Goose Lane Editions

Edited by Phil Hall.
Cover and page design by Julie Scriver.
Printed in Canada.
10 9 8 7 6 5 4 3

Library and Archives Canada Cataloguing in Publication

Blythe, Ali, 1976-, author
    Twoism / Ali Blythe.

Poems.
Issued in print and electronic formats.
ISBN 978-0-86492-873-3 (pbk.).--ISBN 978-0-86492-800-9 (epub).
--ISBN 978-0-86492-844-3 (mobi)

    I. Title.

PS8603.L98T86 2015   C811'.6   C2015-902837-X
                                     C2015-902838-8.

We acknowledge the generous support of the Government of Canada, the Canada Council for the Arts, and the Government of New Brunswick.

Nous reconnaissons l'appui généreux du gouvernement du Canada, du Conseil des arts du Canada, et du gouvernement du Nouveau-Brunswick.

Goose Lane Editions
500 Beaverbrook Court, Suite 330
Fredericton, New Brunswick
CANADA E3B 5X4
www.gooselane.com

Contents

Hotel

Each time you leave me
I pour myself into a drink or
someone else and travel
to the hotel I've built.

I finance it through
unconscionable means.
I lie in bed and watch
the window screen

the same dirty scene.
Tiny people use
tiny rooms to get off
or take off. In the penthouse

someone is doing a terrible
thing to someone they love
mesmerized by a golden
figure waking languidly.

I will apologize later
for letting this happen.
Step back from the window.
Everyone can see.

Pareidolia

This old alarm clock has a sad face.
But I am highly trained to see
sad faces everywhere.

The sad bellhop brings
Freud's letters to Fliess.
I recognize paranoia

from 1895. I am sad.
My mother is sad and
my mother's mother is sad.

So are the best friends
because they "love their delusions
as much as themselves."

Here is a drawing. Though it does not
bear much resemblance to a sad face
I can identify one.

This face has not yet burned
into my toast but the shocked
face in the electrical outlet

powering the sad ticker
spooks me. It is me
who has caused all this.

Button

My doorman once told me
the story of a sage
whose terse enigmas

all sound like *Come with me.*
Upon leaving home
to become a hermit

the sage invited
into infinite solitude
only the gatekeeper

who guarded the edge of the city.
When the doorman finished
this touching story I pushed

the elevator button with my mind
by imagining I glowed yellow
around the edges just like it

and said, *One day*
we will leave this place for good.
Then I swept slowly upward.

Two

I lie with my cheek on the carpet
and peek underneath Two's door. Two lies

on the floor too, watching for monsters
in the ceiling pattern. I locked the bolt.

Two will never be one of those predators
that lurks in bathrooms with ambiguous desires.

I slip Two hormone blockers.
Two's matchbox build is psychology

disconsolate, lonely and invisible, hugging
the poor old radiator for heat. Two is so cute.

Five Letters

Sometimes the inconsolable clouds
clear and I take my orange juice
to the roof. The view is mood-
dependent with a chance of a crash.
I watch invisible enemies deliver

contagious packages all over
my future, which today sparkles
like neurons or sun on the ocean
but with infinitely more order.
Someone left the paper up here

but has already taken their invisible
ink and encyclopedic knowledge
of the omitted and filled in all the
answers to the circa 2011 crossword.
So I make my own that looks like this:

Across
1. Hamlet's papa
3. Wu-Tang face killah
4. ee's hist whist little things
5. As a vapour, gibbering and whining
6. My kind of town

Down
1. *Come On All You* _____ (s)
2. Not much of a chance
3. Write (for)
4. Blinky, Pinky & Inky, for example
5. Don't finish this word, James Thurber

Then I read about the current fourteenth richest
person in America who went public
helping people collect our faces. I have

not yet learned this secret law of attraction
but I sip my juice with a glowing

ball of health inside and think
about the Dutch artist who learned
to make actual indoor clouds
that dissipate even as one admires
their understanding of existence.

Playing Dead

I play dead to trick you into
going about the motions of being
deeply at work on my chest.

Your hair spilling over me.
Your shirt flying open, a lab coat
in a wind machine.

While you are going at it
I really do slip off, a letter landing
in someone else's mailbox.

Thousands of years previous to this
a silkworm cocoon finds itself
in a world of hot water

and begins to unravel
in a prized teacup.
The removal of material

rather
the movement to immateriality
is minimally invasive

for the misnamed moth
plucked between finger and thumb.
A little heap of translucence.

Let's Together Quietly

The future builds monsters
with microscopic locks.
Cancer cells. Click.

I am not here.
I am patrolling the future
in a lab coat

putting an ear
to every numbered door.
Each door has a framed

sepia photo of someone
looking into a camera
and laughing at the person

behind it, who also has a door
and a photo and a person.
Let's together quietly reach

the end of this thought
process and go get breakfast
no matter what time it is.

We'll take the lenses from
our lovely eyes and have coffee
one sugar just how you like it.

Transgene

Eyes are next to impossible to operate
properly. When you undress
I pretend you have not engaged

your top secret anti-scrutiny shield.
I abruptly look at the bird-shape
on the ceiling. Also my hands

are made from the duskiest rabbit fur
thus to keep you from jumping
when I touch your arm and ask

if you'd maybe like to watch
a movie where super transgene
creatures are manufactured

from accidents and go on
to battle the blackest
aspects of their psyches.

Right after the movie we take each other
and laugh because we once again
try to reperform the procedure.

Roden Crater

Oh religion, go away,
stop reminding us of everything.
Since 1974 James Turrell
has been turning a 400,000-year-old

volcanic cinder cone into a massive
View-Master. It took 1.3 million
cubic yards of earth to shape the crater.
The artist is fundraising to finish the job.

When it's complete, people will travel
deep into tunnels and become
empowered by the sun, moon and stars.
They will look up from their cramped

headspace and see a window
that frames what already is
but transports them out
of themselves and into the sky.

Four

Under Four's hunting jacket
an owl and a fox wrestle.

Four's neck is scratched red.
We have been wrestling too.

In the doorway, Four is getting hot.
I offer to hang up the small jacket.

Four tells me, *I can't
let them get away like that.*

I am the fox and Four is the owl.
Then Four is the fox and I'm the owl.

How lucky we are to have this game
to keep us from our adult sadness.

Fox

I stole this one for you: "The fox
never found a better messenger
than itself." But here I am
watching you like a campfire

and wanting to pin you down.
Let me be your woman, your tail's
exquisite nose along my thigh.
Let me be your favourite boy, I want

to tame you. Come closer. I'll comb
burrs from your coat. I'll make
a dish of crayfish and rabbit. We'll play
masters and hounds, you choose.

You have stolen all my hunger.
It's nightfall, please don't go.
Vulpes vulpes. Warm egg thief.
Hocus pocus. Heat.

Owl

I lie on top of the hot sheet
but night air is another hot sheet.
I can hear an owl. It is feeding
another owl.

Mice pour liquid-boned
through my every thought.
Please come prey on me.
Life has gone

dangerously pelleted.
Hard to make out.
The woods are after me
as much as I am after them.

I'm making that up.
An owl doesn't need
anything but itself
and an opening.

Owl says, *Owl is sky,
and you, the weather.*
Make me a light breeze
is all I'm asking.

Hit

Today there is nothing
on the radio in my head
but the hotel radio is playing
"Drops of Jupiter" as my nausea

waits by the tracks for the rush-by
to stop. Being in a train or a Top 40
is like being caught in a lion's
mouth that is still moving very fast.

I know I can't really put on
a body other than my own.
And I know I can't wear you forever,
sick blanket, or you, animal coat.

Children and doctors
are precise with their removals
of the heart and other
unmentionables. I am,

after all, alive, with a hint
occasionally of their fluttering
knives. When sense stops
coming through and the station

overruns with static
I get a rubbed-the-wrong-way
backlit feeling that is high
and whipping like the wind

reading Monday's paper.
Not much in it if it comes at all.
I hope something is about to
pick me up in its mouth and run.

I Am Not Scoring Enough Points with You

I understand the blazing
head of St. Jude. Another
sunny day bashes its club
against my non-mattress ear.

It's going to be a throbber.
I am learning to turn
thoughts into infinitely
re-orderable code-bits

of square singularity
but my mind wanders
romantically
as I crack. While I wait

to remove this sick blanket
and have my turn with you
I stare at a showroom model
of the woods. It hangs

crookedly and lights up
with that marauding sun.
Everything is loved there.
The hound loves a master

and the master races
around half horse half
swathe of English glory
in dappled paths

pounded with hoofbeats,
which is what you actually
see in the painting.
Everything is itself

and not itself, everything
is always itself.
The red fox that loves
to make an escape.

Scintillating Grid Illusion

All day I carry a full grown husky
in my mouth. And every evening
we go to the abandoned kiddie
park to track elusive smell-trails

of night-blooming dog pee.
I watch myself being lifted
by a dad figure to the big pink
elephant. You know that trick

where ghostlike spots are perceived
in the crosses of a white grid
on a black background and disappear
when you look right at them.

People have disappeared
because after a while I looked
through them. The stars are sinking
now with us in their teeth.

Ten

Ten is in my bed. Ten's shirt is off.
Ten could care less and pretends

the sheets are liquid by making
a summer rippling motion from

hips to chest. Ten is a lake-headed
two-thing. A gender-gender fish.

Ten often tells me about being lifted
from the utter, the wider, the water,

and imprisoned in a land of knife-edge
eyes that slit then dressed Ten in a sick blanket.

One-Way Intake Valve to Crazy

I am built on the sinking sensation
of looking back and becoming
aware that the life I long for is just
a larger version of the life I am in

which has only ever been
the leaky dock my whole family
has lived on since the beginning.
O *Leaves of Grass*, remember

when you were slim and beautiful?
I remember when my mother hung
a mirror at the end of my bed
so I could practise. I named the faces

after machines — "The Typewriter,"
"The Blender." *It's all a matter
of how you classify*, Linnaeus said
from his hometown, Småland.

Good Morning You're Awake

It's umbrella weather
in the leaking plywood
tunnel of the chest.

Good morning, my unattractive
tendency, I've made coffee.
I guess I'll rouse you like a nail

then hammer you back in.
Nobody eats breakfast anymore.
Would you like some juice?

I unplugged last night's power
tools. Their shamed orange tails
drip and spark. Sometimes you

look so small, askew, held together
with one pin
I'd like to spit across this room.

You remind me of an article
in *Animal GQ,* "How to Stay
Beaten Broken & Beautiful." It says

the real fun is use and abuse.
"Start with a skin you love then
wear it to the ground."

Rush Hour

When I'm alone in bed, which
happens sometimes, I don't
wear anything but *Clairaudience*.

This means I lie perfectly still
with my limbs and hearing aligned
at the correct angles and become

a sliding door for crystal-clear
messengers bringing dishes
and glasses filled with air.

The sky is also tossing its keys
in the bowl with big silver flashes.
Again the Acute Care Team

rushes the corridors. The radio in
my head. Code Blue.
I have it tipped together just so.

Loose Ends

Last night I remembered
this morning would happen
and took a bottle to the hotel's

predacious recording devices.
You know we have these, right.
Memory takes a hard hand

to its stubble. Last night. I can't
contemplate my shirt buttons.
Assemble, creatures.

Over-cooked coffee. Daily turndowns.
This is your standard-issue accommodation.
The constant banging

when I'm locked in the bedroom.
Refusing conversion and medicine.
Let me out.

Telekinesis has left me
and I must move myself through
our suspicious divestments.

Paraphilia

Your disguise cloud
is about to be whipped off.
The contents of which
are what exactly.

I'm full of the storm
coming. Naked in your
vague walls. Suggestive
in the drugged seat.

Jupiter circles Io. Is this how
it's supposed to go.
You are captaining forever.
I can't take leave.

Shattered

Your eyes look like
beach glass fresh
from a pounding.

I wish I could float
you inside an empty
bottle and raise your

many tiny sails.
But one has to accept
the tense of a feeling.

You will never be
well enough again
to exist on anything

but a diet of thin ice.
You will recurrently
have the sense someone

is checking the time,
which you suspect
might be suspended

from nurse-clean clouds
by a delicate gold chain.
You will have to drink

meds from a plastic
cup. Next, you won't
remember a thing.

Thirteen

Thirteen is on the cot next to my bed
experiencing the rapid shallow breathing

associated with gradual application
of python-tight chest binding.

I too want to travel in reverse.
To un-receive

the regalia of Thirteen's known
symptoms. Thirteen is unable

to respond. I am trying. With
this mouth of lake and insect.

Thirteen can't hear my felled voice.
Feel the soft upraised hands

of my time-moving machines.
A twin sheet suspended between us.

Coming Down

My dentist, before committing
suicide, told me the pain
in my mouth was the undescended

lust of a young man. I am
coming down like something.
It strikes fear in you.

The un-eventuality process:
I have held yours open
with mine for hours

begging removal.
Eventually someone has to
call the whole thing off.

I care for you. You can eat the dissolving
pill beneath my tongue.
This is fingers vs. carotid medication

in which I never cease joining
the cloud above your head.
To remind you of my presence.

Shiner

I'm leaving you.
To take the phantoms
for a walk.

*Everywhere I step
is death* — this comet thought
chalks me with Eros.

Like that shiner
I got for nothing. Your face
steals the light

when you take it
in your lips. There was a time
we could polish

each other off.
It was more beautiful
than I make it out to be.

Golden Time

If you require diagnosis, every indication is
that the careful prescription pads of your feet
move along my glowing aisle markers. I can't

save you, I have no exit. *Save yourself!* I cry
as I smell the fearsome inside of your hat, I will
steal every piece of you. I am able to survive

the ninety seconds of golden time following any crash
with contents from my overhead bin including
headache pills, perfume factory, mini-you.

Theatre

The plastic tray on my bedside table
looks like it belongs in some future
operating theatre. Right now it has
arranged left to right a pair

of nail scissors, a smashed plastic lid
whose agony face speaks to me, three
hairpins pulled from your hair by my
lips last Saturday and a sentence I cut

from the *National Post*: "— they're Caesar
and Rome all over again." I don't know
what that means but I have a feeling
I am about to, so I've kept it.

Everything vs. Everything

This is what it feels like
when I am with you once again.
Listen to the southern slurring

of the good-looking kings
and brothers from music city.
I promise I will

remove the repeat
button from the stereo and me.
We both have the stadium smell

of a good rock concert.
The territory in my brain
is on someone else's territory.

You Animal

Humans make
terrible
lie detectors.

Polygraphs
don't chart lies
but gauge arousal.

You can't hear
a sound for miles.
Except a heart pulling

its dark,
sexy little
rickshaw.

Mask

In the vast ocean
of repetitive
undertakings

my thoughts part
for you and keep
a you-shaped hole.

I take the hole
and put it
on my face.

From this deeper
nullity
I'm watching.

Charge

Your lovesick mother climbed inside
a wooden cow. The world blacked out.

The position of your mother was prone.
Outside, your confused father mounted.

A white bull-ton. Light entered
with every thrust, a milk-sea scent.

When you were born
you skewered a sky hole.

Your boyish hips slipped through.
Starry One! your mother cried.

~

I tell you the same story
to soothe your mounting

hunger — hands clasping
your unwieldy head, shielding

the miscreation tonguing
spume from breast — for one

must eventually accept one's own
sustenance or starve.

~

My black half-ton.
My wrongly hung.

My sweetly familiar
two-in-one.

If only you could batter
the pain, channel

meaning from horn
and gore but you lunge

into the frustrating give
of cloth, fury

becomes a stabbed stagger,
a passing nudge.

The ending
opens before us.

~

Theseus is one of us
you know.

He's immensity.
He's ultimate trans —

suffering on the orthogonal cross.
Hybrid from the hop.

He's Helen, he's Jesus,
and he's aroused. His knee

in your groin. His big fingers
looped with beauty's mercenary

string. Sword lifted, twisted
into your buckling.

~

My anvil-headed.
My willow-hipped.

My little-left-
dangling.

Let me drape like myth
over your long nose

and give like cloth
to fear's charge.

Everything Moving without Me Moving

Night is a diesel tongue
licking salt from the air.

Stars try for a steadying thought.
You relocate me

to the docks and use ropes.
No hope of anything getting through.

~

We're sliding, fly-by-night
and dripping in wet-with-it

seamlessness —
I am perpetually woozy.

The floor leaks
and gives, you have me

by the neck
don't stop I'm so close. Keep

your hand there.
Whatever your hand finds there.

~

In your grip I flash briefly go black.
Then you are all around

all around and moving
like warm over ice

in the shakiest glass.
Shuddering engine under me.

~

I have given you my hands.
You are making use of them.

Like Narcissus come to the water
finding nothing but water

you plunge my hands again and again.
Your dislocated face searching

an inch from mine, and you won't
stop, can't stop until you've hit bottom.

~

We were bottomless
weren't we. I tell myself

the same story over and over
to keep awake. The one

where night goes missing
between us. Remember how

you promised it wouldn't
come to this. The first

light good and punched
sleepless blue, our bashed lupine

skin and you, lying there, skinny
as a cattail, nude. Inured.

~

Eyelashes swept shut.
The shuttling

behind your eyelids.
The hunt for the soft bird

of your own reflection
flushing from the shrubs.

~

Those are my calm hands beside you.
My neck lifting, eyes you dug out,

torso turning, pushing me down,
making me a mirror for you to want

to breathe on. Inside my skin
you have me practise diminishing

until I am the ounce
you keep.

~

Here's where the quiet expendability
of the body genies from the bottle.

I am all the time wanting
to be pulled open

by your thumbnail.
Nothing I do belongs to me anymore.

This is how I move now.
Trees in slow motion trailing the wind.

The Real Rescue

It isn't *always*
about orifices.

But I am the lunatic
sliding fingers in.

Those medicated waters
open, I enter.

Shirt, a resplendent drag.
Those long-board shorts.

A young Hermaphroditus
undressing in the pool.

I become heavenly.
Come heavily.

~

O child with
the nymph

dripping from
your unmuscled thigh,

hardship softened
by delight,

transformation
is disappearance

in Ovid's and every
part of the woods.

~

You go for a walk at ten,
twenty-nine, thirty-eight,

it keeps happening.
You are fifteen and take off your clothes

to drown. To try and put
your body back on.

They pull you from the water
and dress you

right before the real rescue.
You wake in the doctor's office

where someone holds the legs
of a songstress open with a tabloid.

~

O child, I love both
your birthplaces,

they are mine too.
Ovid once told me

you were an unusually
handsome boy —

it was this water
that jangled the rest loose.

~

I dream I pull a razor
from the water. It's worn soft.

I dream in Futanari.
Thousands of intersex

dementias fall in my glass, break
lightly on my chest.

As time passes and returns
to the undistinguishing dazzle.

To the taut scent
of sex and chlorine.

A Small Dress

You push open the door
I smell coffee and wake
slowly telling you I dreamed
you were a small dress
of infinitely breakable sticks.

*I am going to try you on
now*, I said in the dream.
Even knowing what patience
and care it took to piece you
together last time.

A bare bulb made cagey
shadows of you as you
were lowered over me.
I tried not to move too much.
It wasn't a dream, you say.

Any Way We Go Here

I think of our bodies I do.
Their roads going below
to toss. I think of it softly

then not so. I think
of the muscle minutiae
and flinch. When I left you

on the roof, the stars were cold
and clear, their sharps
disposed of in my side.

When I left you in bed
I must have put a first foot
on the floor, I must have kissed you

and slipped off. It's early
or it's late. I'm cold
and a little bit drunk

so am in the shower —
I must have decided something
finally about getting warm

and clean. It's too late. I'm in
the drain. I can't get clear.
The roads. The stars.

It's early days
still. The sharps slip in and out.
The bodies are everywhere.

Goodnight

Every wish is a paw
and I'm the dog attached.

It's too late for any of us
to be better than we were.

Without a shadow of a thought.
Without a single human want.

Goodnight lost causes.
Goodnight desperate cases.

Goodnight, it was a beautiful
day we had nothing to do with.

It could all spook.
Any second now.

Elusive Structure

The only thing I really fear
is becoming *illutible* — an old
way of saying "unable to be
washed away."

Today I give clouds the pet name
Voynich Manuscript
after their mysterious flowerings
in unknown languages.

We could go missing too
as beautifully as Leda or McQueen
who float past me in swan wardrobes.
It's people like them

who run a whetstone along
our pain until there isn't
a whetstone left. Did I tell you
4:30 p.m. on Tuesday has assembled

itself into yellow reflections.
Clocks are elusive structures.
Whenever I look at the time
something isn't about to happen

but my body, being the worst
kind of elusive structure, still
tries to go after what's already
lost to me. For example now

it's 4:31 on Tuesday.
Saint-Exupéry said, "A cloud pile
ceases to be a cloud pile
the moment I begin picturing

a cathedral or a mythical woman
being wholly taken by the rush
of a feathery god."
In soft colours made real

by Agnes Martin's linear
minerals I become and become.
I am sorry. I'm sorry to those
who will find nothing left of me.

The Umbrella

To survive I have to believe
everyone precisely arranges matter
in their environment so it speaks
correctly. Circa right-this-second

I am placing the future you
in my perfectly unappointed
room with the numerals
on the door by typing

minuscule code into a glowing
handheld campfire with my thumbs.
Soon it will rapidly become
impossible to separate

what is happening
to my body from what
you are doing to it.
The inclined gaze

of your occasional attention lifts
a vial to the sun. There is a golden
suspension-fluid and glinting
in it are many floating

and uninhabited one-milligram
chairs. Are there enough of me
to sit in these hundreds
of chairs. This very much feels

like the place you delay yourself
for transport by air. Waiting
abstracted and dreamy
to prescriptively avail yourself

to the next small and human
checkpoint where you're
asked — as we will be all our lives —
to become see-through

for the safety of others. A poet
I loved problematically
and then who left
swiftly from this world

with a terrible burst
in the brain was first able to teach
me that I *should* stand under
the umbrella with the insanely

attractive messenger of popular
music if only to be protected
however briefly the persuasive
notes fall. Out my window

a pilot is performing an everyday
heavier-than-air manoeuvre
drawing one exalted line
in the softest graphite across

all my interpretations, and I
think, *Come down, beautiful
thing, you are running out
of light.* Then I move

a little more this old torture
device that allows you and me
to live in intimate notes
and may somewhat eternally

suspend what's left
of this goofily inadequate
space-time capsule
you like to call by name.

Mise-en-scène

In Luc Besson's best movie
everything wears the big blue
lens of sadness associated
with never getting to go

to the beautiful destination
you every day buy a ticket for.
Our regular feature involves
two chairs and occasional

drifting eye contact. The plot
is where the curtain comes
down and no one brings up
the house lights. I can't

see your hand
but the ice-rattle tells me
you might need another.
Neither in this scene

though we might feel like it
is the long rope to the ocean
floor the two friends dive down
to see who can last longest

without oxygen. Finally
the winner realizes no rope
is ever long enough. One friend
returns to the surface to die.

The other never resurfaces.
The audience is left to wonder.

Acknowledgements

In acknowledgement of the traditional territory of the W̲S'ANEC', Lkwungen and Wyomilth peoples of the Coast Salish Nation, and the Blackfoot, Stoney Nakoda and Tsuu T'ina Nations, where my desk and dreams are situated.

With deep thanks to Lorna Crozier, Kate Douglas, Kim Gilmour, GM & GF, Phil Hall, Elizabeth Hayes, Danielle Janess, Lisa Lewis, Tara Lindsay, Tim Lilburn, Garth Martens, David Seymour, Melanie Siebert, Dr. Liam Snowdon and Anne-Marie Turza. And in remembrance of Michael Cullen.

Much gratitude to the publications in which versions of these poems appear: *Baldhip*, *Descant*, *EVENT*, the *Malahat Review*, *Matrix Magazine*, *The Nub*, *Plenitude*, *PRISM International*, *RockSalt*, *Sand Journal*, *subTerrain*, *This Magazine* and *This Side of West*.

This book was helped along its way by friends, family, colleagues, everyone at icehouse poetry and Goose Lane Editions, the University of Victoria Department of Writing, the Banff Centre and its donors, the Pratt and Short families, and the Lambda Foundation.

Ali Blythe completed a residency at the Banff Centre and a writing degree at the University of Victoria, receiving the Candis Graham Writing Scholarship from the Lambda Foundation for excellence in writing and support of the queer community.